The Red Kite – key facts and figures

Weight	800 – 1,300g (2 – 3lbs).
Length	About 60cm (24 inches).
Wingspan	150 – 170cm (5 – 5½ feet).
Sexes	Usually indistinguishable, though females are generally slightly larger and heavier than males.
Old names	Puttock; glede; fork-tail; crouch-tail. The child's toy was named after the red kite.
Eggs	Pale with irregular reddish-brown markings; about the size of an average chicken's egg. 1 – 4 (usually 2 – 3) in a clutch.
Breeding age	Most first-time breeders are 2 or 3 years old; one-year-olds breed occasionally.
Life span	Average life span about 10 years. Maximum of 26 years recorded in the wild, 38 years in captivity.

Breeding pairs in 2003

Native birds	Wales	350 – 400 pairs
From reintroduction projects	Chilterns	177 pairs
	Northamptonshire	24 pairs
	Yorkshire	16 pairs
	Central Scotland	19 pairs
	Northern Scotland (Black Isle)	35 pairs

Birds have also been released in Southern Scotland and a new release project began in Northumbria from 2004.

Introduction

The red kite, with its impressive five-foot wingspan and spectacular plumage, is one of only a handful of British birds able to thrill and delight almost everyone lucky enough to see it at close quarters. Indeed, to the wildlife enthusiast and casual onlooker alike, there are few sights to rival that of a red kite floating lazily over the Chiltern Hills. The red kite's large wingspan and relatively small, light body enable it to soar effortlessly on thermals or float on the breeze with scarcely a single wing-beat.

The world red kite population is only about 18 – 24,000 pairs, almost all of which are found within Europe. In Britain this once common bird was all but wiped out by human persecution and only a small population survived in remote parts of mid-Wales. It has now, once again, become a familiar sight in the Chilterns and other parts of England and Scotland thanks to a successful reintroduction programme.

Kite or buzzard?

The red kite is not the only large bird of prey to have made a comeback to the Chilterns in recent years. The buzzard too has made a welcome return, moving in from its strongholds in western England following a long absence due to persecution. It is possible that the presence of reintroduced kites has encouraged more buzzards into the area, and kites and buzzards are often seen in the air together. The two birds are rather similar in size but the buzzard has shorter, broader wings and a shorter tail giving it a more compact appearance. The red kite's long, deeply-forked, reddish tail, often twisted from side to side in flight, is one of its most distinctive features. In flapping flight the wing-beats of the buzzard are much faster than the red kite and this allows the experienced observer to distinguish between the two birds even at very long range.

The buzzard (lower left) has a completely different shape and plumage to the red kite, making confusion unlikely at close range

The voices of the two birds are similar, both having a rather plaintive, mewing 'peee-ay' call which falls away in pitch. That of the kite is a little weaker than the buzzard, and often more drawn out and wavering, with shorter notes sometimes added to the initial call. The buzzard is generally the more vocal of the two but kites can also be heard regularly in the Chilterns, especially in the early part of the breeding season and when gatherings of birds form in one area.

History

For many centuries the red kite was a regular scavenger around human habitation

Several hundred years ago the red kite would have been a familiar sight throughout the Chilterns, as it was across much of the rest of lowland Britain. It may well have been our most numerous bird of prey, outnumbering even the ubiquitous kestrel. Unfortunately, the red kite, along with many other birds and mammals, was heavily persecuted in the mistaken belief that it was a threat to gamebirds and livestock. Numbers plummeted and by the end of the nineteenth century the kite had been lost as a breeding bird from England. Red kites last bred in Buckinghamshire in the early 1800s, and the last nest in Oxfordshire was near Bledington, close to the border with Gloucestershire, in 1832. From then on, although a small number of pairs managed to hang on in remote parts of mid Wales, only an occasional wandering bird was seen in the Chilterns.

The return of the red kite

In the late 1980s the red kite was considered to be one of the most threatened birds in Britain and Europe and conservation organisations were keen to do everything possible to help numbers to increase. It was realised that although areas such as the Chilterns provide ideal habitat for the kite, natural recolonisation would take a very long time. The red kite is reluctant to breed away from others of its own kind and the small Welsh population, itself limited by cool, damp springs and a poor food supply, was showing no sign of spreading back into England. The RSPB and the Nature Conservancy Council (now English Nature in England) decided to begin an ambitious reintroduction project, which started in 1989.

Chicks were taken from parts of northern Spain which have a healthy, productive population of kites and kept in two specially built wooden pens tucked away in beech woods close to the Oxfordshire/Buckinghamshire border. After a few weeks in captivity they were released into the wild. The Chilterns was chosen because its rich, varied landscape provides all the features that are important for red kites, including woodland for nesting and roosting sites, and a mixture of arable farmland and grassland with abundant food. The rich landscape that makes this area such an ideal place for the red kite is recognised through its designation as an Area of Outstanding Natural Beauty (AONB).

Photo: Ian Carter, English Nature

A red kite being released into the open countryside

Between 1989 and 1994 a total of 93 kites were released in the same area. Some birds died and others moved away from the release site, but many remained in the Chilterns. The first pair bred successfully in 1991 and the population has increased steadily to the present day. In 2003 more than 170 breeding pairs were located in the Chilterns and the total population was estimated at around 1,000 birds. Since 1997 young birds have been taken each year from nests in the Chilterns for release at other sites in England and, more recently, in southern Scotland. At least one chick is left in every donor nest for the adults to rear naturally.

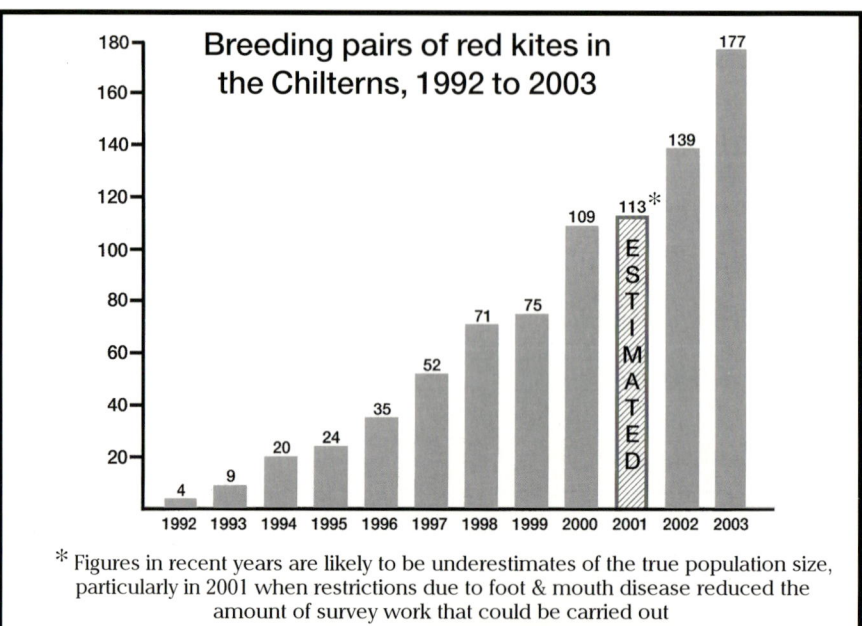

*Figures in recent years are likely to be underestimates of the true population size, particularly in 2001 when restrictions due to foot & mouth disease reduced the amount of survey work that could be carried out

Diet and foraging behaviour

The red kite is one of the world's most versatile and adaptable birds of prey, taking a wider range of food than almost any other species. The vast majority of prey is taken as carrion and any mammal or bird that dies in the open countryside is a potential food source. Small animals are preferred as the red kite is not a powerful bird and has difficultly in breaking through the tough skin of larger species. Even so, in some parts of the kite's range, livestock is an important food source and in Wales, for example, sheep carcasses are frequently eaten. In the Chilterns the most important food includes rabbits, mice and voles, rats, pheasants, crows and pigeons, with less common species taken whenever they are encountered.

The photographs above and right show a group of kites displacing a buzzard from a rabbit carcase. One of them tries to make off with its prize but is unable to carry it away

Kites seen flying low over pasture fields, frequently dropping down to the surface to pick up small items, are likely to be feeding on earthworms, a surprisingly important part of the diet

Red Kites in the Chilterns

Photo: Robert Gross

The adaptable red kite has learnt to exploit road kills as a regular source of food

The rural lanes of the Chilterns provide kites with a steady supply of road kills, especially in summer when young inexperienced animals are regular victims. Kites also take advantage of other human activities including gamebird and pigeon shooting, pest control campaigns and farming operations such as crop harvesting and grass cutting when they feed on small mammals killed by the machinery. In some countries red kites regularly scavenge at rubbish tips but this is rarely reported in the Chilterns. It seems likely that they are reluctant to compete with the large flocks of crows and gulls at such sites and instead make use of more easily accessible food in the countryside.

Despite its usual languid foraging flights, the red kite possesses a remarkable turn of speed and is highly manoeuvrable in flight. This allows it to successfully pursue other birds of prey and crows in order to steal food from them. Kites also steal from each other and spectacular aerobatic displays can be witnessed whenever a number of kites gather at a food source.

Live animals are taken infrequently when the opportunity arises. Small mammals may be caught when they venture into the open, and young crows and pigeons are sometimes taken from their nests.

Red Kites in the Chilterns

Feeding in gardens

While the red kite is certainly not a tame bird, it is has always been able to live successfully alongside humans, taking advantage of opportunities to find food wherever they arise. In medieval times the bird could be found scavenging within some of our major towns, making use of the refuse thrown out onto the open streets. Along with the raven, it was the first bird in Britain to receive legal protection for its valued street-cleaning role. In the Chilterns today, red kites are often seen over small towns and have become regular visitors to village gardens, where many people now provide food for them.

*Food may be taken even from small gardens,
providing spectacular close-up views from the living room window!*

Some people believe that supplementary feeding of red kites is undesirable as it may lead to unnaturally high concentrations of birds and reduce the rate at which kites spread to recolonise new areas of countryside. There are also concerns that butchers' offcuts or processed meat is a poor substitute for the food that red kites depend on in the wild. Kites derive essential vitamins and minerals from skin and pieces of bone, and unsuitable supplementary food may lead to growth problems if used by adult birds to feed their young.

For those who continue to provide supplementary food it is advisable to put out food irregularly and only in small amounts, and use chopped animal carcasses rather than processed or cooked meat. It is also suggested that food is only put out in the afternoon so that birds are encouraged to forage naturally during the first half of each day.

Kites are reluctant to land in confined spaces such as small gardens and so they usually swoop down on folded wings, often at great speed, to snatch up food before carrying it away to a safe feeding perch

The nest site

In keeping with its adaptable nature, the red kite builds its large stick nest in a wide variety of situations, making use of small groups of trees on the edge of rural gardens as well as the extensive Chilterns' beechwoods. Most nests in the Chilterns are in beech trees, reflecting the dominance of this tree in the area, but a wide variety of other trees are also used. One thing that is typical to almost all breeding sites is an easy passage through the trees to the nest, important for such a long-winged bird as the kite. The nest is therefore built either close to the edge of a wood, next to a clearing or woodland ride, or in an area where the trees are widely spaced. Dense plantations are usually avoided. Breeding pairs sometimes reuse a nest from one year to the next, especially when young have been reared successfully. If a new nest is built it is often sited close to the previous year's nest.

Red kites normally pair for life with the long-term bond broken only by the death of one of the birds. Only in rare cases do 'divorces' occur. However, as in many birds, males will take any opportunities that arise to mate with the female from another pair. Early in the breeding season males attempt to

Photo: Carlos Sanchez, rspb-images.com

Red kite nests are usually built at least 15m high in a tree, often much higher, and either lodged in a substantial fork close to the trunk or, more precariously, balanced on a lateral branch

'guard' their mates to prevent this from happening, but the need to search for food means they cannot remain close to the female at all times.

Nest building usually starts in March or early April and this is when the breeding pair is at its most active close to the nesting site. Birds may circle for long periods above the nest wood, calling to each other, and sometimes ending with a vertical dive on folded wings into the woodland canopy. A bird carrying sticks into a wood is a telltale sign of breeding and birds can also be seen carrying dry grass or wool which they use to line the nest.

The red kite has a remarkable habit of 'decorating' the outside of its nest with all manner of rubbish and oddities which it finds in the local countryside. Those monitoring kites in the Chilterns have found disposable plastic gloves, children's soft toys, a pair of tights, bits of newspaper

Photo: N.E.C.Snell

Two of the 'toys' found at red kite nests in the Chilterns

Red Kites in the Chilterns

and magazines, and several pairs of ladies' knickers. Shakespeare referred to the kite's habit of stealing washing hung out to dry when he wrote in *A Winter's Tale* 'When the kite builds, look to lesser linen'. The kite was even known as the 'hat bird' for its supposed habit of removing hats from people's heads for use as nest decoration! The purpose of nest decoration is unclear. No doubt some material is intended to form part of the soft nest lining but becomes detached and ends up hanging from the edge of the nest. It may be that the male is showing off his nest-building prowess to the female or perhaps it serves as a means of advertising to other local kites that the nest site is occupied.

Rearing young

Most red kite clutches are laid in April. Only one clutch is laid each year unless the eggs are lost at an early stage, in which case some pairs will lay again. During the incubation period, the male brings food to the nest or takes over incubation for short periods to allow the female to feed. The chicks are covered in sandy-white down when they first hatch but after about 2-3 weeks the first brown feathers begin to emerge. If food is in short supply, the smallest chick may be attacked by its larger siblings and may even be

Kite eggs are about the size of an average hen's egg. The female does most of the incubation and the eggs hatch after about 30 days

killed. While this seems harsh, it is a behaviour that has evolved to ensure that at least the larger chicks in the nest survive; if the available food was shared equally between all the chicks there might not be enough for any to survive.

Both adults help with rearing the chicks but the female spends more time close to the nest, brooding the young for the first few weeks and driving away potential predators that venture too close. The male may travel several kilometres to find food, which is carried back to the nest for the female to tear into pieces to feed to the young.

Photo: Mike Read

At 4 to 5 weeks old, kite chicks are fully feathered and able to tear food for themselves

The first flight is made at roughly seven weeks but the young remain dependent on the adults for a further 2–4 weeks, returning regularly to the nest to feed. At this stage, young birds that are no longer being fed by their parents may visit other kite nests in the area to take advantage of an easy source of food. The adults from these nests appear unable to distinguish between their own young and unrelated intruders and make no attempt to drive them away.

In the Chilterns, where food for kites is usually plentiful, most pairs manage to rear two or three young. A few pairs rear only a single chick and, very occasionally, four young may be reared in a single nest.

Human disturbance to breeding birds

Nesting kites tend to ignore routine human activities, even within sight of the nest, but they are nevertheless vulnerable to human disturbance, especially early in the season when they have eggs or small young. A kite circling low over the tree tops and flapping vigorously or calling repeatedly is an indication that someone is too close to the nest; the person causing the disturbance should move away as quickly as possible. Eggs and small chicks can quickly become chilled if the adults are prevented from returning, or they may be taken by opportunistic predators such as crows.

The red kite is given special protection under the 1981 Wildlife and Countryside Act and it is illegal to deliberately or recklessly disturb adults or dependent young at or near the nest. To approach a nest in order to gather information or to ring young, a licence is required from English Nature.

Red Kites in the Chilterns

The annual moult

During the summer and autumn red kites are frequently seen with noticeable gaps in their wings and tail due to the annual moult. This protracted process takes several months while the flight feathers and tail feathers are dropped and re-grown in turn. During the nesting period, when there are young to feed, breeding adults tend to have only small gaps in their wings as they need to be in tip-top condition in order to forage and carry food efficiently. But once breeding is finished moult proceeds more rapidly and birds can look very tatty and ill kempt. Gaps in the wings and tail make flight more onerous for the red kite and so, in late summer, they are often less in evidence in the skies, perching unobtrusively for long periods instead. It is fortunate that food is abundant at this time of year as the re-growing of feathers requires considerable energy.

In late summer, moult provides a useful clue to the age of a red kite seen at close quarters. Birds with clear gaps in the wings or a noticeably ragged, uneven tail will be adults part way through their annual moult. Some are so tatty it is surprising that they can still fly! In contrast, birds with immaculate plumage, with not a feather out of place, will be young birds not long out of the nest.

It is not uncommon to find moulted kite feathers on the ground. This collection of wing, tail and body feathers was found in local fields around Radnage during a single summer

Turville Valley – one of the many places in the Chilterns where kites are a familiar sight

Red Kites in the Chilterns

Plumage

It comes as a surprise to some people that young red kites are about the same size as adults by the time they make their first flight from the nest. The wings are slightly shorter and broader, and the tail is shorter, with a less obvious fork than in adults, but such differences are barely noticeable. There are, however, fairly obvious differences between the plumage of young and adult birds and these allow them to be distinguished until the young moult into their new adult feathers when they are about one year old. Juveniles have a duller, more 'washed-out' appearance than adults, with less of a reddish tone to the brown plumage on the wings, body and tail. Young red kites also have a thin, whitish line, formed by pale tips to the feathers, running across the centre of the wings. This is most

These two photographs show the same individual kite (a visitor from Northamptonshire) as a juvenile and an adult. The top picture was taken in January when the bird was only about eight months old and the lower picture was taken in December of the same year, by which time it had moulted into its brighter, adult plumage

Red Kites in the Chilterns

clearly visible on the upper surface of the wing and with the aid of binoculars or a telescope can be made out at a considerable distance.

The differences in plumage between adult and young kites are not so obvious when birds are perched. However, at close range, the drabber appearance of a young bird should be apparent, particularly if there is an adult perched nearby for comparison. At very close range the difference in eye colour can be seen. Adult kites have bright yellow eyes, which stand out clearly against the pale grey head feathers. Juveniles tend to have duller eyes, although they do become brighter during the course of the winter.

Juvenile kites (above) have paler streaking on the body than the adult birds (below)

Social behaviour

One of the most impressive wildlife spectacles in Britain can be witnessed during the winter months in the Chiltern Hills. At this time of year, red kites from a wide area gather together at the end of each day to roost communally. Some roosts involve only a handful of birds but at the most favoured sites more than 200 birds may fly in to roost in the same small woodland. The kite's plaintive mewing call can often be heard at such gatherings and may help to draw more birds into the area.

Opposite page –
Before settling down to roost for the night, kites often indulge in spectacular communal flights, circling around in groups or chasing each other over the surrounding countryside

On calm days when there is no wind to exploit, birds gathering near their roost spend less time in the air and are more likely to perch up in groups, often using isolated hedgerow trees where they are highly visible – like ripe pears on a tree according to one seasoned observer!

The main benefit for red kites in roosting together is related to the bird's feeding behaviour. An individual is more likely to locate a food source if it is part of a loose group of kites foraging in the same area. When one bird spots food, the others quickly converge to share in the feast. The advantage of communal roosting is in ensuring that plenty of birds are together in one area so that group foraging can take place at the start of the next day. Communal gatherings also provide an opportunity for social interactions and it is likely that pair bonds between young birds first begin to form at winter roosts. There is nothing unnatural about the large gatherings of kites that can be seen in the Chilterns; similar concentrations can be found in other parts of Europe where kites are still common. Although the provision of supplementary food can lead to the presence of large numbers of birds in one area, the largest gatherings are at communal roost sites when birds are not actively looking for food.

Red kites are less strongly social in the breeding season though they are reluctant to nest far from others of their own kind and large woods may support several breeding pairs. Nests are occasionally sited as close as 100m to the nearest neighbour.

Aerial interactions

Chases and aerial sparring between red kites are often no more than a form of play - a means by which young birds can test and improve their flying skills. Another example of play is the repeated dropping and re-catching of an object, including small branches which red kites sometimes snatch from a tree in flight for this purpose.

In some situations aerial sparring between two birds serves a more direct purpose. For example, it may help to strengthen the long-term pair bond between birds. Aggressive interactions also occur, especially in the early part of the breeding season when males may try to drive away potential rivals that stray too close to their nest. On very rare occasions two males can even interlock talons in flight and tumble towards the ground as they continue their aerial battle.

Kites are often observed interacting with other species, especially members of the crow family such as carrion crows, rooks and jackdaws. These birds will sometimes mob a red kite, following closely behind and harassing it as it flies past. Up to ten or more mobbing birds may gang up on a single kite. Although this behaviour does not pose a serious threat, it is enough to inconvenience a red kite as it is forced to turn and fend off birds that come too close.

When two or more kites are flying in close proximity, direct interactions between individuals are common. These mostly take the form of aerial chases and sparring, with birds sometimes turning around in mid-air, reaching out to each other with talons outstretched

Red Kites in the Chilterns

Kites often chase each other, sometimes playfully but at other times with more serious intentions, such as to steal food or drive a rival away from the nest area. In this case an adult bird is being pursued by a juvenile

There are various reasons why birds mob red kites. Sometimes it is in the hope of stealing food. At other times crows may see a kite as a potential threat to their young and attempt to drive it away from the area. Often it seems that the crows are simply indulging in their own form of play, improving skills that will be useful when they have young to defend or in attempts to steal food.

Two kites sometimes indulge in a very distinctive, slow-flapping 'display' flight where one bird follows closely behind the other. This may involve two rival males, or a male and female using this ritualistic form of flight to assess each other as potential mates

The red kite is mobbed more than most other birds of prey because its large wingspan and often slow, languid flight make it a particularly appealing target. Here a rook is doing the mobbing

Red Kites in the Chilterns

Wing-tags and monitoring

Wing tags fitted to kite chicks are colour coded to provide information on the origin of a bird and the year in which it was fledged. The main colour of the left wing tag indicates the area in which it was reared – yellow indicating a Chilterns' fledged red kite. The colour of the right wing tag is different for each year as shown in the chart below.

Letters or numbers allow each tagged kite to be individually identified when viewed with binoculars or a telescope. Fieldworkers can gather very useful information by reading wing tags and much has been learnt about red kite movements and survival rates. The tags fall off after an average of 3 to 4 years when the attachments weaken and break.

Some red kites are also given small radio transmitters which allow fieldworkers to follow their movements in great detail. This work has shown, for example, that although red kites often wander over a considerable area when they are young, the majority settle to breed within a few kilometres of the nest site where they themselves were reared. Once a bird has bred for the first time it usually ceases to make long distance movements, spending most of its time throughout the year within a few kilometres of its nest site.

In order to learn more about red kites, fieldworkers from the Southern England Kite Group visit nests in the summer and fit coloured, plastic wing tags to chicks as part of a national monitoring scheme. This bird has a yellow tag on the left wing showing that it was from a nest in the Chilterns, and a pink tag on the right wing, showing that it was raised in 2000 (see illustration below)

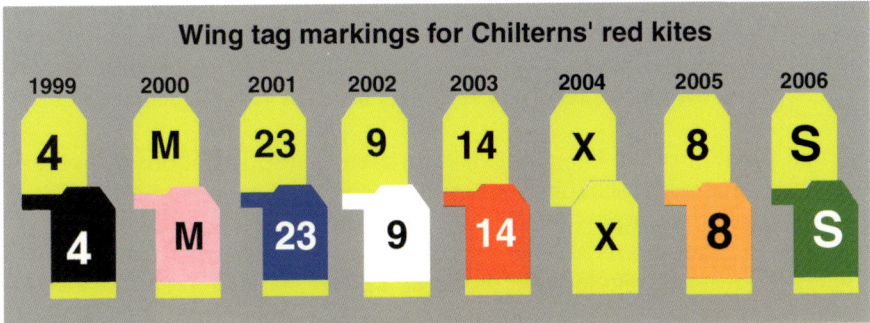

The upper row shows tags for the left wing and the lower row tags for the right wing

Visitors from other areas

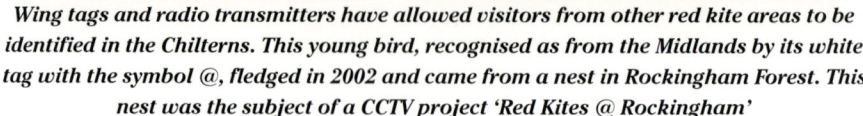

Wing tags and radio transmitters have allowed visitors from other red kite areas to be identified in the Chilterns. This young bird, recognised as from the Midlands by its white tag with the symbol @, fledged in 2002 and came from a nest in Rockingham Forest. This nest was the subject of a CCTV project 'Red Kites @ Rockingham'

A small number of the kites that visit the area from populations elsewhere end up pairing with local birds and settling to breed in the Chilterns. There have also been examples of birds reared in the Chilterns joining up with red kites in other areas. At least two have bred in Northamptonshire and Chilterns' kites are regularly recorded at feeding stations in central Wales. However, most kites that wander away from the area where they were reared end up returning once they are old enough to breed.

Persecution

Despite the undoubted success of the reintroduction project and the popularity of the red kite in the Chilterns, there are still a small minority of people who persecute them illegally. Poison baits pose the greatest threat because of the kite's scavenging habits. Animal carcasses laced with poison and placed out in the open countryside are sometimes used as a means of controlling crows or foxes. They are, however, completely indiscriminate, killing whatever arrives to feed first. Some of the poisons involved are strong enough to kill pet dogs and even humans should the bait be handled inadvertently. The use of such poison baits is a crime that is taken very seriously. Several years ago an individual was prosecuted for deliberately poisoning a red kite in the Chilterns and fined £4,000 by local magistrates.

Photo: Ian Carter, English Nature

A small number of breeding pairs have had their eggs stolen by egg collectors, an outdated practice for which those responsible now risk being sent to prison

Several birds have been found with shotgun injuries and while some have been successfully rehabilitated and released back into the wild, others have had to be destroyed. Other threats faced by the red kite in the modern Chilterns' landscape include lead poisoning (from shotgun killed prey), electrocution on overhead powerlines, collisions with road vehicles and even collisions with trains, though each of these has only affected a small number of birds. Collisions occur when birds are scavenging on road (or rail!) kills and may mostly involve birds that are inexperienced or in poor condition and so unable to fly up quickly when a vehicle approaches.

Problems with rat poisons

Some modern rat poisons, known as second-generation anticoagulant rodenticides, are several hundred times more toxic than the older poisons based on warfarin. They were developed because rats in some areas, including parts of the Chilterns, became resistant to warfarin. Although they are an effective control measure, problems can arise when poisoned rats and other small mammals die out in the open where they can be eaten by scavengers. Both adult and nestling kites have been killed in this way in recent years, sometimes with obvious external bleeding as a result of the anticoagulant effects of the poison.

The red kite is particularly vulnerable to this threat for several reasons. Being primarily a scavenger, kites are always on the lookout for dead animals and a rat is an ideal size of prey. It provides a substantial meal but is light enough to be carried away to a secure feeding perch or back to the nest to feed young. Unlike many large birds of prey, red kites regularly forage close to human settlements and around farm buildings where rats are frequently poisoned.

The threat to red kites would be greatly reduced if people considered using alternative forms of rodent control such as trapping or, in areas where resistance is not a problem, the less toxic, first-generation poisons. Where second-generation poisons must be used, it is essential that the instructions on the label are followed carefully. This includes carrying out regular searches for dead rodents so that they can be disposed of safely by burning or burying. Such measures will not only help the red kite but also other wildlife that is also at risk of secondary poisoning. More information on the safe use of rat poisons is available in a leaflet produced by English Nature and the Royal Society for the Protection of Birds (RSPB), which is available from English Nature's Enquiry Service (see inside back cover for contact details).

Photo: Ian Carter, English Nature

Modern rat poisons are persistent in body tissues and a lethal dose can be built up when a kite repeatedly feeds on poisoned animals. In extreme cases a single rat may contain sufficient poison to kill a kite

Watching red kites

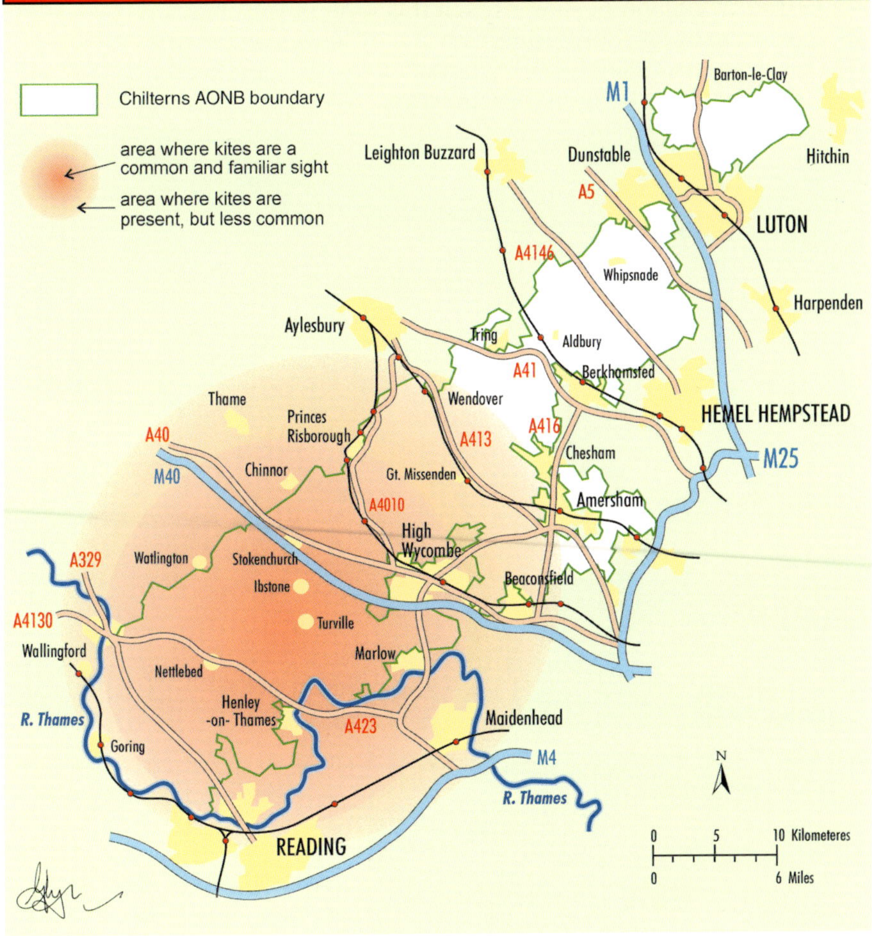

This map shows the areas where red kites have become re-established in the Chilterns. The dark shading shows where they are common and relatively easy to see, with the light shading showing areas where they are present in smaller numbers and so are seen less frequently. Their precise distribution is of course changing all the time so the map should only be used as a rough guide. Some young kites wander extensively and so may turn up virtually anywhere in the Chilterns and surrounding countryside.

Although kites are present in the Chilterns throughout the year, winter and spring are probably the best times to see them. By late autumn the moult is

complete and birds are spending more time on the wing, and as they are not tied to woodland nesting sites at this time of year they are seen more often over the open countryside. The lack of leaves on the trees means that views are less restricted in well wooded areas and perched birds are much more visible when the branches are bare.

Above: **Large numbers of red kites can often be seen flying over the same area**

Opposite page, top: **The red kite is a highly aerial bird, most often seen in flight. It is agile enough to snatch small items of food from the ground to devour them on the wing**

Opposite page, bottom: **Red kites are seen less frequently on the ground, though they do sometimes land to feed on earthworms or animal carcasses such as this rabbit**

Red Kites in the Chilterns